SOUL TRAITS

ANALYSA MARIE

Contact:

Instagram: AnalysaMarie
Twitter: _AnalysaMarie
Email: ContactAnalysaMarie@gmail.com

Book Cover Design:
https://www.linkedin.com/in/angelriveranyc/

To my parents who are always beside me as I go on a journey looking for my place in this world, thank you for finding me when I get lost. To Justice who is always trying to understand my struggles while you are only eight years old thank you for giving me words of encouragement. Only you can turn my sadness into complete happiness in a second. My little family is my inspiration. When I dream you are all in my vision. None of this could have been possible without you. Thank you.

Thank you for all of your lessons. I have turned them into blessings.

To everyone who ripped the love out of my chest,

You have taught me the beauty in the ugly. I was a product of pain and misery. At this point I couldn't remember the girl I was before I drowned in an ocean of depression. I was not strong enough at the time to fight off the people who had such a tight grip around my life. I basically gave them the power to lead me into a depression for six long years. Growing up I was surrounded by love, but of course there was always a part of my life that was not secure. I believe the many rejections I will face later in life stemmed off of a person who helped create my life. I don't give this person a title because to me he is nothing but a sperm donor even though he literally was not a sperm donor. At a young age I experienced the abuse he used to create such a broken home. He was the first person to create such horrible images in my mind. He introduced fear to me. When I was a really young girl I remember having nightmares of him and at such a young age I understood that a father wasn't supposed to be a villain to his child, but I also understood that, that's just who he was and I knew I didn't care to have him in my life even when he denied me. I didn't grow up looking for him and wanting to be accepted by him. Even with all the negativity he has created in not only my life, but also my mother's. She always made this broken home feel whole. I never felt like I was missing any love from my life and I never searched for more love than I was already given. Since a little girl I have always looked up to my mother in hopes that I could be as strong as her. I always appreciate that she is the woman she is because our situation could have went left and everyday she always made it right. At some point in our lives all we had was each other, but during that time that's all I ever needed. Fast forward my mother meets a man who basically became a God in my life. If I thought I was already healed before him, then I was wrong. He was the missing piece to complete our lives. He came into mine and with no hesitation he took care of me as if I was his own blood. This new life taught me that blood doesn't connect people together. It's the heart and soul that they have. God should have given me to him before I was born because the Lord only knows I wish I could have met him sooner. The lord only knows how much I wish I could have avoided such a monster. I found myself wanting to be like him when I grow up and in many ways he became my inspiration for a life that I was building.

As I got older I have met people in my life who mistreated me and I allowed them to because I grew this hatred against myself and I can't necessarily identify why I never allowed myself to be worthy to someone. The people I met along the way meant something to me and when they didn't value that about me I would completely break and look for others to put me back together. All of these people who claimed to care about me was not there when I needed my weak body to lean on them. I have spent late nights crying until I couldn't breathe and I have kept myself alive during those nights I didn't want to breathe. Overtime I swam up from the ocean of depression and I saved myself. I don't give credit to anyone who fixed me, because no one did. I did. I give credit to the people who weakened my heart because they taught me how to be stronger. For all the days I have lived in pain, I now deserve to live a life of peace, so I forgive you all for ripping me apart. I am now complete.

To everyone who is at their worst in life, I promise you this pain will pass. You will be your own superhero. All the rain that has poured down on you was just helping you grow. This is your time to heal. Get ready to take power over your life again.

If you were not here with me while I was in the dirt, don't be here with me when I grow.

I am not scared to feel pain again because I have witnessed all of this beauty that comes out of the struggles.

Lately I've been kissing my curves that you rejected because you were too afraid you would get lost in them. I am feeding my mind with seeds of love when all you have ever done is blow my petals for your own wishes. You have excluded me when all I have ever done was give you parts of myself I should have saved for someone who is afraid to break me. You have scared away the woman in me when I've been teaching her not to fear anyone who didn't give her life because they couldn't take her life. You have stolen the beats in my heart and now every function in my body is breaking down. It feels like I am lying still on a ground while everyone around me is moving to the rhythm of life. You have given me aches instead of comfort, you have made my head spin too fast to think about the love I was taught to allow into my life and you have drank my blood to give you life. You ruined me. You ruined me in ways that even waves can't do to a person who doesn't know how to swim. I am waving my hands in the air in need of saving. You have made me fall in love with silence because only when it's quiet I can focus on you while you forget about me. At this point I'm just bones who's too afraid to walk away because I will break. The only cast to heal me is your hands when they trace against my wounds. I am convinced I will forever be half of the whole I could have been with you.

I am tired of people saying I have changed because I no longer try to find healing in the pain they bring upon me. I am now discovering the woman I am so I can have enough strength to look past those who leave me in the past. I am no longer looking for places to hide. Instead I am finding comfort in the places that once were too hectic for me to stand. I am growing into the woman I have always dreamt about and now I'm keeping my eyes open so I don't miss her progress. I am learning that I feel everything deep in my soul but my heart is protecting me and not allowing me to act out my deepest feelings. Some days I am frustrated with teaching myself all of the lessons I need to learn to survive life and I pray someone will come along and show me which paths I should cross. But I understand that I will only learn their lessons and it will not help me in my own life. Sometimes I feel like I am crazy, but life can get crazy and it's okay to be insane sometimes. If I was ordinary all the time, then how will I be able to write stories out of memories that are the same everyday. I now know that loving the wrong people isn't a mistake because everyone we loved, we were meant to love as lessons. I understand that energy is contagious and I shouldn't surround myself with people who murder spirits. I am only searching for people who bring me peace, I am releasing myself from a cage for the people who make me feel free and I am no longer holding myself back from falling in love with people who don't see the injuries in falling in love with me.

Stop breaking your own heart. The glow from your happiness is missed. I know it's probably hard to remember the times when genuine happiness defined you. You used to love the light that the sun fed you, but now you close your curtains when the hottest ray tries to kiss your skin. Don't let the definition of pain be your name. You are glory, you are salvation and you are worthy. Your pain is not here to break you. This pain is here to rebirth you. Your skin will shed and power will grow on you. You will fall in love with yourself all over again.

I made a home out of myself and no one is worthy to
spend the night.

Understand that love is not always meant to look pretty. Love is messy and beautiful. Sometimes you are going to be the beautiful half and they will be the messy. Vice versa. But life is about balance. There's a reason it's called the perfect match.

If you have been fighting a battle with someone who is toxic in your life and you have walked away from them, you already won. Once you realize that you deserve to be treated with respect and love, then you are already a step closer to nurturing your body, mind, heart and soul. A lot of people stay in relationships that are hurting them more than helping them grow because their love for that person is the only thing they know and if that's taken away from them they feel that they won't be able to function properly. If you continue to stay with this person you are only allowing them to think of you as an easy target to hurt. If you give someone multiple chances they will never change. At this point you can't get angry with them because you are the one who is allowing this poison back into your life. They will continue to do wrong by you because they know you will always be there to take them back. You have to love yourself enough to be able to walk away from anyone who does not love you. Understand that you were brought onto this world for a purpose and that purpose is not to fulfill a person's life that is not even worthy enough to be in your life. Don't give them the power to think that they have power over you. Let these toxic relationships be a lesson in your life. Let them remind you for the future of whom you should allow into your life and whom you shouldn't allow into your life. Educate yourself on these experiences so you are able to identify the wrong signs and be able to walk away from it. There is someone who is made for you. They will love you and respect you, but before you find that person, you have to be that person for yourself first.

Don't listen to society when they tell you that you need to lose weight. They're only feeding you unhealthy thoughts. They discriminate instead of teaching the world how to be healthy. Instead of ripping women and men apart, they should teach us all how to treat our body with respect. They should use the power of their voices for the right things. Not to bully us.

Not everyone is going to love you as much as you have learned to love yourself. I need you to take a moment before you let your heart break because of the opinions of others. Think about how long it has taken you to get to this level of comfort with yourself, then ask yourself is it really worth letting someone take that away from you in an instant. You can't let others control how you live because if you do, then you have already failed yourself. I know in this generation people beautify another person swooping in and saving you from yourself, but I promise you the only hero you have is yourself, so treat yourself the way you wish others would treat you. Be an example of the love you always dream about.

I learned something about selfish people over the years. Even when they know their love and concern for you is fake, even when they know they will abandon you, sucking all the trust you put into them out of you they will still enter your life just to taste the sweetest parts of you and of course you will hold the door open for them because your heart is much bigger than theirs. Once you are no longer useful for them they will spit out that taste of sweetness they once craved for and they will leave you with nothing but an aching heart while their heart still beats with life, but one day reality will hit them and they will realize that you never lost them, but they simply lost you.

We need to surround ourselves with people who make us feel every emotion we can possibly feel. As individuals who prefer to stay to ourselves we tend to hang around people who are safe because we are scared to emotionally feel and we don't want anyone to bring out our feelings we have spent so long trying to protect, but we need to connect with those who bring out a side of us we are hesitant to expose. We can't continue to limit ourselves to the greater things in life that are calling our names. We only get to live once and as time progresses we don't want to regret anything we should have said or should have done. Experience how life helps you grow. We should live this life with people who are crazy about the beauty of this earth. We have to learn ourselves and by doing this we will find ourselves and with finding ourselves we will accept ourselves and with accepting ourselves we will become comfortable with leaving our marks on places that can only be identified back to us and because of that people will fall in love with our thrill.

I am alone because they have all heard that my mouth only speaks of his name and the only thing they have learned about me is him.

In the beginning I didn't see that God has put you in my life for a reason that goes way beyond a broken heart. God has given you to me for a lesson that teaches me to never weaken but only strengthen after going through hell with a person I thought loved me. God put me in your life to show you that your greatest loss will always be me. You will crave a love that will feel far too familiar to you and your mind will trace back to me. Your heart will feel empty and the only person that can fill that void is me. But I'm already too full to allow you to make my solitude overflow.

If you wake up with the intentions of making the day beautiful, then I guarantee your day will be a good one. I learned the days that I was dreading I had to do something for myself in the morning that would make me happy. I feel that we get too busy in life that we often forget to take care of ourselves. You have to be able to pick yourself up when you're slugging and tune out anything that holds you back. You have one life and you don't deserve to not want to wake up in the morning. Your intentions should become purer, your mindset should become strengthened, your patience should be exceeding and your outlook on life should be nothing but a positive point of view. I always say if you aren't able to see a change since the last year, then you aren't growing. Make sure you take a lesson out of every situation you step into and carry that lesson with you as you experience new days and don't forget to make the next day better than the last. It's always important to say you're further than you were yesterday. You should be incredibly grateful to live this life. Make it something you've always wanted it to be.

Don't expect a person who has been nothing but toxic in your life to turn out being the healthiest thing you think your own doctor would recommend you. Once you allow someone to disrespect you the first time they will just continue disrespecting you simply because they know you will continue to take them back into your forgiving heart. They will take advantage of your love for them, but your tears and your pain means nothing to them but just a game they love to play. Stop allowing yourself to be a contestant in their game because after every round you're going to lose and the only one walking away with the gold is them. You can't change a person who does not wish to be changed. Everyone does not have the same definition of love however when someone genuinely loves you with all their heart and all their soul they will never purposely put you through pain, they will never keep you up at night questioning whether or not you're enough for them. Once you come to terms what real love is I promise you will fall asleep with dreams instead of waking up because of nightmares.

There are going to be days you are going to need his shoulder to cry on but she will be leaning on it. Even though you need someone you won't dare to make a fool of yourself and call somebody to cry your heart out to because you know you will only run back to him so he can tear you apart some more.

Girls need to support girls. We are the only ones who know all of the things that make it hard being girls and only we know the reasons that make us love being girls. We need to stop hating each other because of boys, we need to stop being jealous of each other and we need to stop competing with each other. Instead of pushing each other down we need to catch each other when we fall. We are all beautiful in our own ways. Our differences are power. We should be placing crowns on each other's heads.

If you can't make a person fall in love with who you are internally, then you lost them. Looks can only get you so far. If you sit in front of a mirror all your life admiring your beauty, you'll forget all of the beauty that comes from a person's heart. You'll miss out on all the beautiful memories two people who connect with each other's soul make.

I have always loved hard and I have always broke. I'm starting to think I should change my reputation to delicate lover. Handle with care. All I've ever wanted was for you to caress me with your gentle hands. But it seems like you will never put your boxing gloves down. You look at me everyday and you can't seem to see all the bruises you have ever painted on me. But that's my fault. I've always looked at you like you were an artist. But I was graffiti on brick walls. Never art hung up in your home.

It's ironic how much love I give to you when I can't even love myself. I'm always wondering how I'm able to love if I never knew the definition of the word. Love has always been missing from my heart, so why does my soul always crave it. It's like you have jumped into my deepest parts and you have saved me, but I'm still praying to God for him to take me. As my blood flows out I am reminded that even this is not enough to keep me alive. I am giving you all the love I could never paint on myself and I'm turning you into art. Your love does not heal me but it holds my hand while I try to heal myself. Loving you is teaching me how I should love myself too.

Continue loving. Love with every beat your heart pounds through your chest. Because when you lose your mind love will follow and cure you. Nothing in this universe compares to the love you radiate towards the ones who love you back. It is the greatest magic I've seen all my life. When you have nothing and when you are empty love will fill you up and heal all your wounds.

You only loved me because you wanted to feel good about something. You wanted to believe you were capable of doing something good. But your love is fake, that's a reflection of who you are. You are not capable of good. You are capable of ruining a good person's life.

Don't criticize and punish yourself when a person is doing wrong to you. Don't let them brainwash you into believing that your love was never enough for them. They will try to blame you for their own insecurities and bad habits. Don't make excuses for them because you will only encourage them to hurt you even more. They don't deserve to be loved by you if they're not reciprocating that love back to you, they don't deserve the effort you put into saving the relationship when it was hanging on a thread, most importantly they aren't worthy enough to know the deepest parts of you. If they never appreciated you, stop waiting for them to see the God in you.

I don't want to be set on you when you are still out searching. I don't want to wait until you get it together within time then, hear how you're sorry because you were too blind to see that I was your remedy for life. I don't want to only be your springtime when I'm blooming beautifully because that is the only thing you can handle. I am much more. I am heavy snow on cold winter days and almost way too hot tempered to cut the flame on a sunny summer day and no umbrella can stop me from the rain I become when I feel pain. You don't get to come back whenever you feel like you should. I had a voice that you tried to silence me of, and wings that tried to fly but of course you had to cut. You blew my petals off wishing for your own dreams to come true. You painted me only the color blue. I was too busy making a king out of you, I forgot I was a queen, and every time you needed me it was my shoulder you would lean on. You were wrong about me. You said I can never live without you but now that I have the chance to breathe, it smells like an eternity without you.

I learned that there's nothing wrong in loving with passion.
I beat myself up about how I should calm down with love.
Now, I know that when you're in love you're supposed to
feel everything to the extreme. There's no point in loving if
you aren't passionate.

You cannot use a woman's flaws against her if she has learned to love each and every one of them.

Be with you again?
I can't even imagine myself thinking about wanting to be with you again.
I'm doing well now actually I'm doing great now. Not that you care because let's face it the only time I was allowed to be happy was when I was with you.
But I was never happy with you.
All the times you had my mind running wild I mean you even had control over my dreams.
It was like every ticking second you were there to remind me of who you were. Like you were some damn trophy.
But you're not. You're more like aluminum foil you crumble the second too much pressure is put on you.
I prayed to God so many nights to make my love for you disappear because deep down I knew how sick you made me.
When I was with you I felt caged in.
Now, I found the key and I feel so free.
I feel so free that I can stand on the highest mountain and just scream because that's how powerful I feel.
I have control over me when for so long your hands were wrapped around me with the tightest grip I couldn't feel my blood circulating anymore.
The boy I'm with now actually you were the boy I was with, but the man I'm with now makes me blush and gush with emotions.
He makes me feel so beautiful.
You just made me hate myself.
I looked in the mirror and it's like I had to find a way to make myself look attractive that your mouth will just start watering every time you looked at me.
That's my fault.
I made you too hungry and when you starved I was right there for you to devour me.
All you ever did was make me weak.
But now I'm strong.
I'm strong enough now to look you in the eyes and say I don't love you anymore.
You were all wrong.
I got too caught up on wanting to see you win I let myself fail.
You taught me one thing in all the years we were together.
You taught me that the kind of man I deserve isn't you, but the opposite of you.
But most of all, the biggest lesson I've learned is that I had to reach myself, I needed to love myself more and love you not at all.
But just know you didn't win.
You walk around so proud to have all these broken hearts in your hands but you lose.
You lose because you lost a girl who saw heaven in your eyes when really it was hell

I hope she's worthy of your love. I hope she learns that no matter how strong you tend to be there are times you want to crumble and you won't allow yourself to. During those times I hope she lets you make a home in her arms. You are not always an open person and I hope she understands that it's because you have endured pain. I hope she doesn't take advantage of your fear. I hope she undresses your mind because you have one of the most beautiful and intense thoughts. You always bring others back to life. I hope she's worthy enough for your saving.

God,
I still pray for him even after he broke my heart.
I'm starting to think that I should pray for myself because
you only know that I'm the one who is in need of healing.
I fell to my knees as the bullet hit me and I formed my
hands together and I'm asking you to save him, keep him
safe, make sure he never feels weak.
That's love...
The love didn't go away the moment my heart ripped in
half.
It took awhile for it to patch and so soon for him to laugh
and think of me as a joke.
I can't fall asleep without talking to you about him because
somehow I feel like I'm talking to him.
Lord please let this man see the light, I know he must be
tired of the dark.
You have been giving me signs that I've been too blind to
see.
It's like he was a suspect and I couldn't choose him out of
that line up because he's my life line.
But he killed my spirit and maybe he should do the time.
So I push him away, no matter how bad I want my body to
be intertwined with his.
God, I wanted to save him and be the one to catch him
when he falls.
But I've fallen a thousand times and I'm tired of people
asking how those bruises formed.
But they'll never go away because God, the only one who
broke me can fix me and I've lost him a long time ago.
Is it wrong for me God, to wait for him to tell me that he's
coming home because I've been lost ever since he left.
I just need to be in his arms, I need to be kept.
Amen.

We rip each other apart instead of using this love we have created to put each other together. I can no longer remember the reasons we have fell in love with each other and I'm not too sure if we are still in love. Instead we aim words at each other because we know where it brings the most pain. You have become tired of my cries, but I only cry because I've noticed your grip on my hand has loosened. I want you to remember me. Look at me and remember why you fell in love with me in the first place. Remember how we started fires with both of our passions for each other. Don't leave me. Tell me this love is worthy enough to fix. Tell me this is a love you'll always miss. Lately this love has been making me feel a wreck, but if that's what it takes to keep you, then I will turn this into a beautiful mess.

She will try to love you with poetry in hopes that she can make you forget all of the lines that I have written for you, but little does she know that I am the one who made you fall in love with poetry.

We were made differently from each other for a reason. That's how we learn from others. We learn from others by how unique we all are. If we were the same, then there wouldn't be anything to really talk about, or new things to fall in love with. Never question your worth. Never look in a mirror and get frustrated with your reflection. Stop looking at girls you want to resemble, more importantly stop trying to resemble them. There are people who look at you with such admiration. Please don't change who you are. This world can't afford to lose another rare individual. You add character to this universe.

You are worthy of everything you believe you deserve. Stop lowering who you are as a person to fit the standards of someone else's dream of what they want you to be. Don't ever lie in bed at night wondering what you can do to make yourself lovelier. You are already beautiful the way you are and when you learn to love that, no one else's opinion on you will matter. Kiss your flaws and learn to love them. They say perfection doesn't exist but when you learn to fall deeply in love with yourself and you look in the mirror you will see it was possible all along. You are perfect.

Lately I've been trying to teach myself how to breathe without you. I've been trying to find the meaning of life since my meaning for life left me. The only rhythm my heart knows how to beat is from your love. I keep telling myself my heart will be put back together within time, my mind will soon forget the memories and my skin will learn to survive without your hands. You should have never ripped me apart if you had no business in cleaning up the mess you made. Love is supposed to create and if it didn't then you and I wouldn't have been formed. Your love only killed me and now because of you I understand the meaning of a broken home.

When you are at the stage of going through a breakup with someone you really adored you will tend to believe that no one can love you the way they have loved you. If you were with someone who is toxic to you, then you should actually be happy that you wouldn't find another person like them. You need to realize their love for you was never true to begin with. If you continue to have this mindset through life you will never properly heal in a healthy way. Understand that no person should have the power to shatter you and no person should have the power to make you view love in a different way. When you are ready to move on, make sure you aren't moving on to get over the person you were previously with. That will only hurt you more. Jumping from relationship to relationship can be poisonous to your heart. You need to give your heart time to heal. Take the time out for yourself to learn more about who you are and come to an understanding with yourself about what you're looking for in your next relationship.

The first night we met you showed me stars in the sky a city girl like myself has never been able to see. You made me believe in all my hopes and dreams and even though we were only temporary we were figuring out our whole lives together that we would only live separated from each other. You always gave me your hand even during the times you were collapsed on the floor. I'm not going to say we had a beautiful love, but we had a real love and that's what made others admire us. That's what made me admire us. You have accepted me for everything that I am and everything that I am not. You took my fears away. I am no longer afraid to get my heart broken because you taught me the kind of man I deserve. Because of you I have learned to never settle for less. That night you left, I shattered in a million pieces but that's only because you were the one keeping me together this whole time. You made me feel safe and unbreakable. I hope you find happiness even if it's without me. You're my superhero and I mean that in the most innocent way possible. Your love will forever be written in the palms of my hands that once fit perfectly in yours.

Don't tear apart the pieces of yourself that you hate.
Understand that those pieces put together your beauty.

You bring silence to my head full of thoughts. Thank you for being my peace

I figured out that no one's love ever completed me. It only made me more alone than ever. I had to learn that I will never find love if I search for it and I will never find love if I settle. If I do, then I will never find a love that's as powerful as mine. I will only find a love that's genuine when it finds me and when it sees that my love is just as powerful as theirs is.

As much as you broke me, disrespected me and forgot about me. I do not regret you. You have taught me what I truly am worthy for in life. You have taught me of all the warning signs to avoid.

You're going to know when you find your soulmate when your connection with that person overpowers the beats within your heart. You will get this feeling of certainty that no one has been able to make you feel before. There's something inside of you that lights up and let's you know that this person was made for you. As time goes on your connection with this person will never weaken, but it will strengthen. Things will not always go right, but with the strong bond that is shared between soulmates any conflict can be solved. A soulmate will never have you second-guess whether their love for you is true. Instead you will just know that their love for you is raw and you will be at peace with it.

You are what I've been praying for. You are what I was made for.

Stop wishing pain and regret on the person who broke you. Move on, wish them the best and when you see them, walk with your head high. There's no need to check up on an ex if you're looking for a connection that's been lost a long time ago. How do you expect to grow if you're watering dead situations? There are people out there who are meant for you. Take your encounters with the people you have met and let that guide you to who you should surround yourself with and who you shouldn't and if you find your relationships are ending the same, you need to change who you invest your time in. Always level up or maybe you just have to change your mentality and actions. Level up your mindset as well.

How long are you going to look at all the places in your home you both scarred your love at? Go outside and buy yourself new pillows and blankets if you can't get rid of the thought that he once laid here, erase the love that was made here, go save yourself. I know your heart is weak and your mind is rotting but you are harming yourself when he is not alarmed by it. The world is not in flames but you see it as if it is in ashes. I know you fell deep in love with the person who made you feel complete when you already thought you were, but look deep within yourself and you will see you were all you needed to survive. You were breathing and living life before they made a pit stop within your heart. I know it seems like you aren't enough to get through another day, but each morning when you wake up I promise the sun won't burn you anymore. You will fall in love again with the things this heartbreak took away from you. You will feel whole again. Your heart needs you to be strong.

If you have to ask someone if they love you, then you already got your answer before you even had to ask

You sucked the sweetest parts out of me. I didn't give you permission to taste what God poured into me. I didn't want you to know me like that. I can't trust another person. I cried out for help just to be told that my screams were too loud. I don't know who to turn to. I feel defeated. I know I can't continue to blame myself for your mistakes but I feel guilty for not being able to save myself when I was drowning. You have stolen my identity, you have stolen my purity, and you have stolen the little girl that was always inside of me. I have failed that little girl that was counting on me to protect her. I've never searched for love again because you took that feeling away from me. I hope others see that the monster in me was created by the monster in you.

There have been times when I was not happy with who I was. I always had this constant thought of wondering why I couldn't have been made into the person I wish to be. I would constantly look in mirrors and pick myself apart. I was not happy with the girl I was. She was never enough for me. It got so bad that I truly believed there was no point of my existence. I was set on the feeling that there was no purpose here for me. My everyday life turned into this routine of breaking myself down. I had to start forcing myself to think about completely different topics to occupy my mind from entering my darkest thoughts. It soon became easier for me to accept this pain I was feeling rather than boosting my confidence because again I believed I had nothing to be proud of. I built this safe haven in my room because it was the only place I was able to be away from everyone. I didn't want anyone to be in my presence because I didn't want them to stare at me for too long because then they will see all the ugly I see in myself. You would think I would feel the most comfortable with myself while being alone, but I didn't even find comfort in that. Even when I was alone I tried to look the most beautiful and force myself to feel beautiful even if I knew it wasn't true. I have allowed the thoughts of others to control the thoughts I had on myself and this turned into a sickness. I needed to be saved from myself. I didn't have anyone to seek help in because I pushed everyone away. I made sleep my best friend, food my enemy and happiness was just an unknown language to me. I became okay with allowing myself to break my own heart. I didn't care to allow love into my life. Every time I would watch the sunrise I just wanted to see the sunset and I don't know if that was a metaphor for my life.

Growing apart from the people who were once closest to us isn't always a bad situation. When this happens we become very hurt because we invested so much of our secrets and vulnerability with them. I'm sure they have invested a lot into us as well. This is bitter because we have to close a chapter in our life that we became used to. People outgrow each other. We are all changing and most likely we are outgrowing the things that initially started the foundation to this relationship. As life goes on we sometimes aren't able to give the person what they need in life and they aren't able to give us what we need in life either. Only we know what's best for ourselves and only they know what's best for them. Instead of being with a person we no longer have a connection with its best to remove ourselves from the relationship and start a new journey. There shouldn't be any hard feelings. Just accept it for what it is and understand that it's part of life.

My stretch marks show me how much I have grown and how far along I have come. You cannot tell me my journey to self-love is ugly.

I don't feel anything. Right now I am empty. I don't regret anything, I don't hate anything and I don't love anything. I am not pushing you away because I am mad at you or lost interest in you. I am pushing you away because I need to be left alone. I need to drown in my sea of thoughts. My soul is calling out for some one on one time and I need to feed this to them. If I don't, then I will never grow. I don't feel like my life is progressing. I just feel stuck. At this point I don't see myself gaining anything. Everything I have put my life into I am losing. I put all my trust and love into people I see potential in and I receive nothing back. I am not saying I give to take, but I am only human and if I'm giving you love, then I need to receive love as well or else this situation just becomes exhausting. A relationship was never meant to be one sided to begin with. It's not fair that I give my all to people who only paint over me. I will still be here. I am real. I don't feel bad for your anger towards me for leaving when it seems like you never cared if I stood to begin with. I have outgrown you and everything else in my past. I am shedding off my pain and I am entering a life that is healthier without you. I am not asking you to apologize to me and I am not asking you to change for me. Instead I have decided to accept the person you are. I am empty like I said I was, but I am going to be full of love that I will pour into my life. I am creating a life of love. Your misery is not welcomed here.

If my future self could have spoken to the broken girl I was in the past I would have showed her the woman I have made of me.

Let me tell you what's the saddest part about this love. I have lost myself in this love and I have never searched to find myself. What was traumatic wasn't the way you loved me but the way I never loved myself.

Gain your self worth, so you can gain an idea of what you truly deserve in life.

I find comfort in being alone with myself. I have spent far too much time taking care of others, it is now time to heal myself. I am learning who I am and sculpting myself everyday. Who I was in the past and who I am today is just an outline leading me to who I will grow into in the future. Love revolves around me first and if I don't spend time to love myself how will I teach others to love me because the way you love yourself is the way you teach others how you need to be loved. Sometimes I steer through life, making the wrong turn and I end up lost, but I never need anyone to look for me because I will always find myself. I have searched for the world in others just to find out there is a universe within myself.

My depression led me to find comfort in being sad. As soon as I would feel happiness I would shut it out because it was an unfamiliar feeling to me. One day I woke up and I became tired of this dead person I created myself to be, so I planted seeds of love within my body, mind, heart and soul and I began to blossom. When I started to put myself first things in my life started to fall in place. Everything that was hazy to me soon became clear. I learned that the only person who can save me is myself. Once I stopped depending on others and started depending on myself, I have never been let down again.

When you first fall in love with a boy you might fall in love with him even if his heart isn't made of gold. He will most likely push your buttons to see how far he must go to make you crack. He is preparing himself to hurt you and see how far he should go. Chances are he will exceed that limit. You will take him back into your arms. He will take away the glow you once admired about yourself and he will make you settle for half love instead of full. You will still give your all because your love either comes all at once or not at all. One day he will leave you for another woman and it will catch you off guard. You will run to the bathroom to puke out all of the hurt and regret you are feeling because of him. Know that you will be the only one cleaning up after a mess when he didn't get dirty at all. But when you first fall out of love you will become more powerful. You will never allow yourself to fall over a person who has no intentions on catching you.

I will only be the woman you need from me if you can be the man I need from you.

Love can make you feel like it is too much for you to handle. But understand this, love is a balance and sometimes you are going to have to pick up their mess and show them the beauty in it. Sometimes you are going to have to be their air when they can't breath. You need to be prepared to drown when their tears have no limits and you're past the borderline of floating and about to sink. You need to count the stars with them and show them the beauty of the night when they have been so used to waiting for the sun to burn it away. This is love. Love isn't always easy, but if you truly do love them the way you say you do then you need to be able to inhale them without having a chest full of regrets.

I remember when I was depressed a long time ago and the thought of death didn't scare me. I am now praying to God thanking him for letting me see another day. When you fall in love with life you will be scared to be taken away from it and that's when I knew I healed myself. That's when I knew it was worth saving myself instead of looking for someone to fix me. Life gets better, don't take yourself away from it.

I have gained
and
I have lost
either way I remain powerful

I've walked into relationships not being confident in the person I am. From day one of the relationship I would fear losing this person to a better woman or just losing this person because I wasn't good enough for them. Those types of situations taught me that I was never enough for myself. I didn't believe in my love enough to not only love someone else but also love myself. I had to learn that I am worthy of everything and my heart didn't deserve to bruise because I didn't think I was valuable to let it pump. How can others put their heart in my hands if I don't even know how to hold my own?

Some days I wake up hating the body I'm in and some days I wake up loving the body I'm in, but it's gotten to the point where I'm loving myself more than I'm hating it. I'm different and everything about being different is okay. The best advice I can offer is love who you are because once you love yourself, you won't care about others negative words towards you. People will feel the love you have for yourself and they'll love you too. I feel like people try to fix their physical appearance too much they let their mind become weak. They ignore the most important part of themselves and that's who you are inside. Once you're mentally healthy and learned about self-love everything in your life will fall into place. You won't allow the negativity you don't deserve into your life. I swear you will wake up with more smiles instead of depression.

If you decide you no longer wish to keep me in your life, then I will not chase you. I no longer care about losing people who do not wish to be kept. I have brought myself to a place in life where I don't have the energy or the cares to love a person who does not want to be loved. Understand that you can't break a person who has constantly shattered and put themselves back together every time. I refuse to tear myself apart to make you feel whole. I don't depend on others to make me happy because that kind of happiness will only disappear as fast as they walk out of my life. Yes, I am selfish when it comes to my happiness, love and life because I have seen how much power I hold and I know that I am rare. Not everyone deserves to know the deepest parts of me.

I know my body is curvaceous and I probably shouldn't wear what that skinny girl would. I can't even imagine the looks I would get for that outfit. Clothes always looked too seductive on me, so I always found myself over layering because I didn't want others to misinterpret me for the woman I really am on the inside. Usually boys judge me from the outside and they never make their way into my mind. I'm always being told that having curves is a good thing. The reasons for it always have to do with a boy. I don't understand when people are going to learn that a woman's body was not created for another person's pleasure. When will boys understand that women's bodies are not pit stops, when will women stop allowing these men to only visit their bodies. I am not here to give myself to you. I will not allow you to take from me. Learn that you will only find a good woman if you get to know what makes her a good woman.

I know it's hard to let go of the person you gave your heart to. I know all you are left with is tracing the parts of your body they have touched. I know you are constantly remembering the feelings you felt in that moment their fingers traced your skin. I know you have seen your whole life in their eyes. I know how it feels like when your whole life has crumbled. I know it's hard when you believed this love was steady and they slipped away without a caution sign in sight. I know you want to believe that if it's meant to be they will find their way back, but deep down you know if it was really meant to be, then there would have been no reason to let them go. I know you think you can't survive without them, but I also know you will feel more alive without them.

I remember the night he told me I would be better off dead. This is a person I have seen the universe in. I believed in him and I let him lean on me during the days he wasn't able to pick himself up. As time went on he began to make me question not only his love for me, but also my life, so when he said those words to me I spent the whole night contemplating it. I didn't understand how this person felt so comfortable with letting those words slip out when all I have ever done in our lives together was praise him. I came to the conclusion that he hated women because he was battling personal issues he had within himself. I just hope he takes his failures and he turns them into blessings because no matter how hard someone hits me I cannot crack. In other words I will wish the best for you even if you do not wish to see the best for me. I hope you recognize that your presence hurt just as much as your absence. You can pretend to be happy but fake happiness is the worst sadness. You wished death and pain upon me, but I wish you find life. I wish you find the beauty in it and I wish you learn to love it so you are able to love yourself.

Don't beat yourself down because you finally agreed to get out of a bed that carried you when you were too weak to hold yourself up. You are brave for continuing on when everyone gave you every reason to want to give up. You don't have to put on a fake smile to make others laugh and you don't have to pretend to be happy so others can feel good. Heal in your own way and heal on your own time. I just hope you don't lose yourself in the waves of depression. I hope you come back as the person you once knew and if not better. When you get to where you want to be in life, when you learn to love who you are, you are going to see why life had to pressure you. You are going to understand why you have to feel weak in order to grow stronger.

No means no. It doesn't mean to convince me and it doesn't mean to beg me until I say yes.

I am not sane without you. I am surrounded by planets looking for my star. I know you're starting to see a world without me. I need you to remember why our love grew. I cut your heart open to learn the deepest parts of you. You cut my heart open to watch me bleed from the pain. You wanted to mark your territory and I still licked the blood off your finger.

I'm trying to hate you as much as I forgive you for all of the things you do to me. All of the things you do to me I should hate you. I'm only hating myself right now because after all the pain you have put me through I am still by your side cheering you on in this game I'm always losing. But I'd rather lose the game instead of lose you. I know this isn't love but I fake it because somehow when I go to sleep you still make me feel half full. The other half of me is floating in air trying to reach out to you so you can be just as high on this love as I am. I want you to be just as addicted as I am. I want you to hallucinate when I'm gone the way I see you in my dreams and wake up to emptiness.

When you grow you reach a level of strength no one can tear down. When you make mistakes or you go through any situation that is difficult it will not affect you as badly as it did in the past. It's because of the growth you have gone through stages to achieve. During that process you will learn that there is always room for improvement and these mistakes that you face are only lessons to better you as an individual in your journey leading to the future. Never take advantage of the power in your development. You will always rise higher than your downfalls. You teach yourself how to love the parts of life that are hard. You will learn that your wounds are what make you stronger and when you understand that you will no longer fear to become scarred again because you know you will always come out fiercer. When you become broken you will always heal yourself and you should be proud for teaching yourself how to become your own savior.

Don't disrespect women when you exist because of a woman.

I've learned to be completely in love with myself. Not in the form of cockiness, but in the form of strength. Instead of looking for someone to be my muscle when I was weak I decided to accept the challenge of not letting anyone break me simply because I was so happy with myself anyone who didn't love me the way I love myself wouldn't be able to bring me to ruins. I have become very careful of who gets to experience me. I don't want anyone who is not worthy being able to know the deepest parts of me. How you love yourself is how you teach others to love you. Love isn't perfect but love always means respect. The moment you see how precious you are is the moment you put an end to anyone trying to harm you.

You are worthy of finding a love that kisses your soul.
Never allow a person to chase you for your body that was
created to create life. Do not give someone the power to
break your heart that your mother took nine months to
grow. I know it's always the people who are willing to rip
their heart out of their chest to keep the ones they love
alive, who end up suffering, but please never turn cold
when your touch was meant warm others. It will sting when
they have sucked all your nectar out but remember your
nectar created their honey. You have fed them the love
they lack. You have made them whole.

When I am with a person it's because I am able to see a life with them. I am thinking long term. I don't believe in getting involved with a person if I know it's going to be temporary. My time is very important to me so if a person enters this relationship with me and their intentions are to not be serious, then they're not only hurting me, but they're also taking away the time and emotions I could have spent and given to someone who was on the same page as me. When I meet new people I like to be open with them. I like discussing old relationships and old situations. Typically a person wouldn't consider this to be healthy, but I believe it's going to bring two individuals to an understanding on how we want to be treated. We often jump into relationships without the proper communication and that leads to failure within the relationship. As your partner I want to understand what broke you in your past and what healed you. It's not about being bitter towards their past lover. It's about understanding why they are the person they are today. We often forget that these people act a certain way based on previous situations. They just didn't turn into the person they are overnight. When you're falling in love you should be open with your partner. There is no need to hide anything. You should be able to talk about and do things without feeling like you're going to be judged for it. You can't be scared to give them your all. Share your secrets and show them the deepest parts of your life. You can't expect to find a relationship that is real if you can't be real with each other.

Not everything you plan will take you to your dream destination, but when you get lost you will sometimes find a home in the things and people you weren't originally running towards. You will be relieved that life had better plans for you.

I never talk about him because he was the first person to lead me into a life of being broken. He turned my innocence into ugly and my heart full of gold to be rusted. He is the reason I am not so trusting towards people I encounter in life. I learned that I couldn't treat everyone the way he treated me. I get what I give. If I enter a relationship with my guard up, then that person will only keep his guard up as well. I wanted to not feel a thing the way my heartbreaker did. It would anger me that I allowed this person to have control over me even after the relationship ended. I was tired of being in a dark place after feeling pain and I was scared to feel that again, so I tried to numb myself and I just became very cold towards the ones who wanted to love me the way I should be loved. It took me time to understand that I had to be in that painful situation to learn from it. It was teaching me that there are people who are for me and there are people who aren't. If you give me a negative sign that I saw in my past relationship then I should only allow myself to witness that sign one time instead of sticking around to see the second time. I think that's one of the keys to figuring out if a relationship is for you is by looking for the signs and acting accordingly. If you're not being treated the way you should be, then you need to get yourself out of that relationship before you end up at square one trying to understand where you went wrong when you should have learned from your past to understand that you shouldn't allow a person to wreck you. Love is meant to be beautiful and love is meant for two people to build each other and build a beautiful foundation. If a person is doing anything opposite of that, it's a waste of time and you need to stop giving people chances because your heart shouldn't have to deal with constant pain. It needs to be nourished by you and by others.

When you're going through pain it's best for you to grow through your pain in the comfort of your own presence. During this process is when you need yourself the most. Don't allow temporary comfort into your life. Don't let anyone distract you from strengthening yourself while facing your pain.

Every time I learn something new, I also learn that I don't know everything. I am forever learning and I embrace that this world has so many lessons to teach me. I will grow from this. I will use these lessons to benefit me.

Love will always be a message we need to listen to
because love overpowers any other language.

Don't let the people who hurt you make you view others as heartbreakers. Everyone is different and everyone deserves a chance. Let people prove to you that they may be different. You can't judge everyone because of your painful experiences. People can always surprise you. If you allow your past to control your future you can be destroying many healthy relationships and people who only want to do good by you. Don't become the people who have taken you for granted. If you believe everyone is the same, then you're only limiting yourself.

Because if you don't love yourself, then who will? When you start to see how much you're worth and should be valued you will see a change in the people who radiate towards you. If you love yourself, then there would be better people in your life who will love you the right way. I'm not saying every person will love you right, but you have to be able to put an end to anyone who takes you for granted. Love who you are, inside and outside. Never degrade yourself. Not everyone is going to be passionate about you but when you're in love with yourself and you're at peace with who you are internally and externally, you will not be bothered by a person who doesn't know how to love you. You will always feel whole even if you thought they were the half to complete you. You have to get past the stage of looking in mirrors to get to the point where you are able to walk past your reflection and you are able feel it in your soul that you are beautiful no matter if others aren't able to see it.

Don't complain about my heart being cold when you haven't warmed me up. Trust me, I don't want to make you freeze, but I need you to understand that at times you make me shiver.

You expected my full unconditional, genuine and raw love when you never loosened your grip around my heart. It burst. I constantly caught myself crying in my bathroom tub because our love went down the drain. Every night you shattered me and every morning I learned how to put myself back together. I accepted the suffering because all the amount of pain while being with you would be much better than the pain I would have to face without you.

I was a rose you picked out of a garden full of daisies. I dropped to the ground as soon as my thorns were too sharp for you to handle.

As long as you keep me in your heart this love will never die. You live in mine forever. We keep each other alive.

Self-love is basically throwing the middle finger up at anyone who tries to punch holes in your canvas and anyone who isn't able to see that failed art class in school. Don't take it personal. Laugh about it, actually pour yourself a drink and then laugh about it. Cheers to that.

People mistake love for pain. Love is what makes the heart beat. It's the people who beat our hearts who bring pain upon us.

Letting go of someone you love is hard, but holding on to them will only make your hands weak and at some point in time they'll slip away. In that moment clouds form above your head and when you cry it storms. You're going to try to aim your lighting at that one person. He broke your heart and it sounded like thunder when it hit the ground, but I swear if you close your eyes, take a deep breath and trust yourself, in time the sun will come out and dry the puddles you've been too depressed to step out of. Trust your strength in the healing process. Don't ever let a man turn you weak. Woman up and the next time you see him smile and give him the best eye roll he's ever seen a woman give and move on because someone else will appreciate the way you flip your hair when you're arguing at 2am about nonsense, someone else will appreciate the way you HAVE to fall asleep in their arms after that argument, someone will appreciate the way you can eat a whole tub of ice cream when you're feeling down and call you beautiful because that's probably the most talented thing they've seen someone do and most of all someone will appreciate the way you love passionately. They will look at you with amazement and kiss you like they're trying to keep a hold of you with their lips that way you won't stray too far away from them. Every heartbreak is a step closer to your soulmate. Don't pay attention to the people who fill your heart up, pay attention to the people who fill your soul up.

Our connection is beautiful. We bring something out of each other that no one else can. I love how the world may see you as one person, but I see a side of you no one else does.

Take my hand I want to go with you. Let's learn each other.
I want to grow with you.

Don't be afraid to take power over your own path in life. People will try to taint the vision you already painted in your head and at times it will discourage you. They will tell you the way you're trying to reach your goals is the wrong way, but it is not up to them. It's ultimately up to you. No one knows your vision like you do, no one has a passion for what you love the way you do, no one knows your potential the way you do and no one dreams the way you do. Don't let anyone control your path to your own success. Whoever is dragging you down instead of helping you stand up shouldn't even be part of your life. This is your purpose. Only you know where you want to go, don't let the traffic get in the way.

If you are constantly convincing yourself of reasons not to let go, then understand it is not worthy to hold on to.

I know sometimes it hurts more to stay away from the person hurting you than to put an end to it. You think that one day all the love you have put into them will be acknowledged and appreciated and they will reciprocate it back to you. But you can't force a person to love you if that's not how their heart decides to beat, you can't force loyalty out of a person who likes to swim in every river and you can't change a person who is perfectly fine with how they are. You indulge yourself with hope and what comes out is loneliness. Don't be blind to see that if he really cared about losing you he would have held onto you tighter. He is manipulating you because you're giving him the power to.

I have gone through life looking for a king to fulfill my fantasies. It took me time to realize that I am a damn Queen, so I placed a crown on my head and since then no one has treated me any less than the royalty I am.

I don't blame anyone or anything for all the hurt I have suffered from because I know I am the one who allowed all of that pain into my life. As years passed by I became adjusted to the comfort of pain. I made this mistake where I made myself a home to toxic people and situations in my life. After much disappointment I tried to figure out why I was the one who would always end up crying myself to sleep, but all along it wasn't rocket science to see that the only one who was hurting me was simply me. It took awhile to see that there was no knife in my back because I already planted it in my heart. I learned and came up with the result that I am the only one who can control how I live my life, so if I wanted to see a change then I had to be my own change. Own your mistakes, but don't be your mistakes. Be the result of what your mistakes have taught you. It's normal to see the light in the darkest people but as long as you learn that you are the sun, you'll never let a dark cloud block your rays again.

I think our relationship failed because we were both broken looking for each other to heal one another. Looking back now I realize it would have been impossible to guard your heart if I wasn't even able to protect mine. I'm not going to say you didn't see how much I was worth because you definitely did but the problem is that we couldn't see the worth within ourselves. We were homeless and we found a home within our broken, cracked walls. No matter how much I was hurting, you always seemed to heal me temporarily and I guess you can say I fell in love with the moments you were giving me but if we're being honest I think we both knew these moments would only end up as memories to us.

Don't numb yourself from feeling. Allow yourself to feel things. That's how you learn, that's how you appreciate, that's how you grow.

To the men who claimed they wanted to love me, but instead didn't want me anymore I have a better understanding of what I deserve in life. To all of my "perfect matches" I will not allow you to put me out anymore. I found God when I killed all of my demons. I have made a lover out of my heart that never wished to beat. I have grown into the woman I never thought I could be.

I don't find weakness in vulnerability. I find it to be brave
and powerful. This is strength.

This is how breakups become messier than they should already be. When a person is disconnecting themselves from you it is because they no longer feel that you are the person they want to bring into their future. They don't feel anything for you, so it's best on their part to let go. By them doing that you basically understand that they have no more time to waste on a relationship they no longer want and you shouldn't want to waste time in a relationship that you are no longer needed in. Of course it's going to get messy because you have invested so much feelings and time into this person you don't want to start over with someone new. But you will because that is life. But this is where it gets even messier. After that person rips your heart out of your chest they still feel the need to keep in contact with you. I don't think we'll ever figure out why these people latch onto us after breaking things off. By them doing this they are now making us confused and now they're making the healing process difficult because we don't know if we should move on or if this broken relationship can still be fixed. This person won't communicate with us about it. Instead they give us mixed signals. So we just take it as this relationship can still be saved. Until one day they catch us off guard with another person who's captured their heart and now we need to release ourselves from this toxic situation once again. We are the ones left cleaning this mess they created while they're out putting together new memories with someone else.

It's your fault for giving me a different view on love. Love doesn't make my heart beat fast anymore and those butterflies in my stomach just flew away. I've been trying to train my body, mind, heart and soul to react to love as if it is going to save my life because one time not too long ago it did save me. Out of all the people who wrecked me, you by far have been the worst. You bled the love out of me and now I am completely numb to the idea. There's this boy I know my heart is in love with but I can't find it in me to love him the way I should. I know soon enough he will find a woman who believes in love the way I once did. It's not fair to break this man the way you broke me. You turned me bitter. I shouldn't have allowed myself to fall into a hole you dug up but I'm trying to climb out of it. I'm afraid if I don't allow love back into my life it might be gone forever. I miss it more than I've ever missed you. You were never worthy of my love, you were never worthy of my touch, and you were never worthy of knowing me. But I hope one day you will learn that with love comes breaking and you will shatter the way you shattered me.

I begged you to save me but you asked God to take me.

If a person tells you they no longer love you, don't make them tell you a second time.

You have taken me into your life like I am holy. Like I am the only one who can bring you to a level of spirituality. You are my baptism. You love me so gracefully and for that I will believe in you the way churches preach. I will lift you up like the man above. You bring me to heaven. I read you like the Bible and trace over your skin like scriptures waiting to be honored. I will always give to you and never give up. You didn't make me fall into a temptation but instead you touched me the way God never touched Mary. You have a hold on me.

My arms are always open for you because I am always
searching for closure in you.

If I had dug a little deeper I would have seen that flowers were blooming from my toes up. Today I graduate from self-hatred to self-love.

My love for you is deeper than these words that I've written for you. Our connection is deeper than the distance between us. I'm surrounded by thoughts of you everyday of my life. And I don't want you to fall in love anymore I want you to grow with this love. Some people come with emotional baggage and I'm more than happy to help you pick yourself up and see your worth. You never took the time out to heal right. You and I see the world from different angles and because of that we disagree and agree when it comes to the topic of our life. I've been in your shoes and it's hard to walk through life knowing you don't see the point in it. You don't deserve to be disrespected or neglected by the people you put your heart into. Never expect anyone to love you perfectly but you do need to be loved with respect. Even though before you I felt so complete, I didn't need love, you still managed to make me feel like I was missing something and now every void in my life is full. No matter what situation you have been through don't let it defeat you. I know words from people don't help the pain you feel. It doesn't help put everything into perspective for you but you need to know you're beautiful inside and out and I cherish every part of you. I know healing is a long procedure but you have to stop depending on people or things to complete you. Some people come along just for a lesson, take that lesson and grow from it, be stronger because of it. No matter where life leads us just know I'm never too far.

Falling in love with you taught me I never knew a thing about love.

You taught him what a good woman is and to match that
he became a good man.

I know you would like to believe that you destroyed me because you're the type of person who gets pleasure from other people's pain, but it wasn't you who destroyed me. I destroyed myself. You were the first one to break my heart, but I am not going to blame you for this one. I am going to blame myself. When I first laid my eyes on you it was not love at first sight. You were actually someone I wasn't too fond of. That is where I went wrong. I learned to love something my heart knew was toxic. Before getting serious with you I was a broken girl that lead me to be vulnerable. I knew what kind of boy you were but because I was vulnerable it didn't take too long for me to fall in love with your words instead of having you prove your actions to me. I wanted to believe that you would see me as girl who was different and you would want to be better for me. Now I know I wasn't much different than the girls you were previously with because if I were I wouldn't have allowed you into my life so easily. I would have listened to what my intuitions were telling me about you instead of making excuses for you. I wanted to believe you would catch me and when I fell I wanted to believe you really did love me and when you decided you no longer loved me is when I learned how to love myself.

I remember I would grip at my body in such disgust. I taught myself not to be hungry. Overtime I learned not to crave food. I told myself once I shed a few pounds I will be happier. Instead I shed the little happiness I had along with the pounds and the only thing that was left of me was a skeleton looking to gain some happiness. Physical appearance doesn't guarantee a life full of happiness. We see beauty in others that we forget how beautiful we are as well. A man and a woman came together to create a human being that they look at as art and we have people in this world who aren't happy with themselves who try to make others feel ugly. You were created with no flaws on your exterior. It took awhile for me to accept that beauty is more than how I look. The biggest compliment isn't "you're pretty" it's "you're powerful." We go our whole life building our character and it's shameful that our appearance is the only recognition we get.

The longer I hold onto toxic people, the longer I will remain in pain.

You loved me the way I loved myself. Not at all.

Closure is just another excuse to speak to them. The only closure you need is that they treat you like you have no value and that should be enough for you to move on.

I'm not saying it is going to be so easy to let go. You created so many memories with a person it doesn't take one moment to walk away. If it was that easy to let go, then chances are you weren't holding on too tight. But I will say this, as days go by you learn to live without them and your pain will begin to fade. Little by little you will allow yourself to release yourself from this heartache as long as you believe in your strength. Understand that one morning you will wake up and you will feel better. We are all human. Never reprimand yourself for feeling too much. You should worry when you don't feel anything at all.

I was the only one on my knees praying for something better than right now. I was searching for me, trying to figure out how this caged girl can be free. I finally escaped out of the crowd of fear and disbelief and I found myself. I started off as roots and I bloomed into a flower. My petals hold power and my stem no longer slugs. No matter how hard a person tries to rip me out of the ground I refuse to ever wilt again.

I often look for relationships with loyalty and security. It wasn't until my mind went on fire that I realized I need a lover who brings me sanity.

I remember praying to God to keep you in my life and when you left I lost my faith in romance.

You are the one I want the most to stay. I write these words in hopes that you will be able to feel me and I don't mean feel me like "I love you too." But feel me in the way that when you want to say you love me you will make me feel your love. Make me feel the way your eyes stay stuck on me like crazy glue when I walk the streets of Manhattan. Make me feel the way your heart beats fast it feels like the world is having an earthquake. Make me feel the way you feel inside. Like no one has ever touched you in the way I have. Like anyone after me will have to learn a new language to understand the stories I have written all over you. Feel me in the way that when you hold my hand you can feel my veins bursting because my whole body is electric and our love can never stop sparking. But it's as if I've known you before I even knew your name. I'm not getting to know who you are, but I'm starting to feel how much I have missed you. All my days without you felt like I was in a crowd and I still felt lonely. It's as if I'm looking into a mirror, but my reflection is moving differently. We are different people, but somehow I feel like our hearts beat at the same pace.

You are going to feel lost sometimes, but you will always have me to call home. We don't need wedding vows. Death can't do us part. I love you for eternity.

I entered a relationship with this boy whom I invested a lot of emotion into. He brought feelings out of me that I have never shared with another person. I was under the impression that him and I would strengthen each other. Now, that I am looking back we were both very weak individuals who didn't have any strength to give to each other. I somehow dug deep into my soul to give this boy something that can help build a bond that was unbreakable. I allowed myself to be completely vulnerable with him because I was exhausted of weak connections with people. I was hoping for us to discover each other in ways no one was really able to before. I ended up getting destroyed when he was only feeding off of these emotions I was being really brave to share with him. I convinced myself that if I taught him how to love, then maybe he will open up and contribute growth to a love that I thought we mutually had for one another. Ultimately he taught me that people couldn't be taught how to love. The key to loving a person the right way is by experience, but before he gains experience within relationships he needs to be able to want to give himself to a person. He needs to be able to want to leave his selfish habits behind. He needs to figure out within himself whether he is ready to give himself to a person without holding back from them. As I came to this conclusion I also figured out that I need to use my experience within relationships to understand that not everyone was made for me which means I need to protect my heart before I become so quick to put my all into a person. I need to make sure they are the right fit for me. Before entering relationships I need to give this person enough to be interested in me and leave them craving to want to learn more about me. I can't give someone all of me right away and I also can't deprive them of myself. I need to enter relationships slowly and test out the vibe between each other before I make such a huge commitment. Love is a feeling that comes naturally. I will eventually know when the timing is right, so I need to stop forcing the time to be right.

My mother told me when your heart beats fast it's because you love someone. That's how I knew I was in love with you. My love for you is growing, I think I need a bigger chest. I was made to always be there with you when the sun rises and you feel like you can conquer the world. I was made to always be there with you when the moon paints the sky and the world has come crashing down on you. God made me for you. I vow to never neglect, and to always protect your heart, and when things get too hard I will never regret this love. I've been living life with only half of me, you came along and now I live life to the fullest. Thank you for picking up all the pieces every time I break. Thank you for showing me real love instead of fake.

You preyed on me while I prayed for you.

It was real because I wanted you more than I needed you.
It was pure. We were pure.

Love is when you accept someone for who they are when they're alone. Love is missing that person when they act like someone else in public.

I hope you understand that what you don't do another person will and if you put me down another person will put me on a pedestal.

When I started a journey with you I lost myself in a world that I shared with you. I forgot what path I was going on before I met you. I always wondered how you were able to remember where you were going before you met me along the way. I forgot who I was and I forgot who I wanted to be because the moment I met you I knew the only thing I wanted to be was your soulmate. I'm only stuck with a forever thought of how you were always the one for me but I was never the one for you. I always wonder how relationships always end up with one person feeling more than the other. We were going through the same things together, but how come it was me who felt more, how come it was you who didn't feel at all. I try not to cry because it's life. I just want to remember the life I knew before you.

We are each other's missing pieces to complete this love that we have both gone through life trying to connect with the wrong people. We tried to make forever's with people who only temporarily fall in love. We gave others all of us when we only received half and we cried to those who made beats with our sounds of pain, but I am not them and you are not them. I will not temporarily fall in love with you and you never make me feel like you love me any less than you did the day before. I will remain in love with you when all of your days consist of darkness and I know you love me even when I don't allow any light into my darkest days. You made me believe in a love that is so pure and so true. Your arms are really strong for lifting me up when I can't hold myself up. A lot of the times I like to believe that I don't need anyone to lift me when I'm down, but when I find myself in the darkest place in life you make it brighter for me. You're my strength when I'm weak. Thank you for being my heart beat. You have poured so much love into my life and never stopped pouring even after it overflowed. Thank you for touching me without using your hands. Thank you for not only saying you love me, but you also put your words into action. This is a love I didn't think I would ever witness. You made my dreams on love come true. If I would have known a couple of years ago that you would be the one to heal me I would have stopped giving myself to people who broke me. You never question if my pieces will cut you, you just pick them up and put me together because that's what love is. Love is messy, but it's beautiful. You don't stick around for just the beauty but you see the beauty in the ugly. I love you for loving me in ways I couldn't love myself. Our love is way beyond two hearts beating for each other but it's two souls becoming one.

I have gone through my life without knowing the definition of what love was. My journey in life was to always find the definition of this feeling that I craved for. Every time I thought I got close to understanding the meaning of love and the purpose it had for life I got shot down with rejection. I didn't think I was worthy enough for love, so I felt myself giving up on love. In these moments of drowning I always had writing to understand why I would feel the way I felt. I came to a place in my life where all of my pain was too heavy for me to carry on my back. It came to the point where I no longer wanted to understand my emotions because writing about it always gave me a constant reminder of my negative feelings. I abandoned writing, so I can avoid confrontation with myself. I didn't want people to view me as weak when they read my writings. I wanted to maintain this image of strength. Later on I learned to embrace every storm that formed within me and I no longer cared about others opinions about me. I let words find me until I felt myself healing. Writing a book has always been a dream of mine and I thought it would always remain as a dream instead of reality because people who were close to me told me that being an author was not a real career. This led me to pursue my studies in Psychology, but it wasn't long until I found myself running back to my first love, which was a pen and a notebook. I have gone through my life feeling like something was missing and it was this book. I had to write this book in order to feel whole. I have suffered in life and I have been blessed in life and I am ready to share my experiences with you all. I am ready to be real with you, so you all can trust in me and feel comfortable enough to be real with me. I have lost the woman in me many times before and I am extremely overwhelmed with happiness that I was able to get a hold of her again. This is not the ending, this is only the beginning. I want to grow with you all. I am no longer terrified to get lost in people. Let's lose ourselves in each other with emotions and let's find each other with intentions of saving each other.

Analysa Marie

Made in the USA
Middletown, DE
06 September 2020

18218532R00077